PAINTING AND DRAWING

PAINTING AND DRAWING

Editorial Consultant:

JUDY MARTIN

A FIRST GUIDE
THE MILLBROOK PRESS
BROOKFIELD, CONNECTICUT

A QUARTO BOOK

First published in the United States of America in 1993 by
The Millbrook Press
2 Old New Milford Road
Brookfield, Connecticut 06804

Library of Congress Cataloging-in-Publication-Data

Martin, Judy
    Painting and drawing / by Judy Martin.
        p.   cm.
    Includes index.
    Summary: Describes different materials for painting and drawing
and discusses how to use them, providing tricks of the trade and
examples of works by famous artists.
    ISBN 1-56294-709-5 (trade ed.). – ISBN 1-56294-203-4 (lib. ed.)
    1. Drawing – Technique – Juvenile literature. 2. Painting –
– Technique – – Juvenile. [1. Drawing – – Technique. 2. Painting –
– Technique.] I. Title.
NC655.C7   1992
741.2– –dc20   92 – 18414
                                                              CIP
                                                              AC

This book was designed and produced by
Quarto Children's Books Ltd
The Old Brewery, 6 Blundell Street
London N7 9BH

Creative Director Nick Buzzard
Managing Editor Christine Hatt
Editor Patricia Seligman
Designer Hugh Schermuly
Photographers Paul Forrester, Ian Howes
Illustrators Judy Martin, Elisabeth Smith, Sharon Smith

The Publishers would like to thank the following for their help in the
preparation of this book: Tessa Paul, Karen Ball, Rebecca Herringshaw

Picture Acknowledgments
Quarto Children's Books Ltd would like to thank the following for supplying
photographs and for permission to reproduce copyright material:
Wayne Lankinen/Aquila: 84 center

Typeset by Central Southern Typesetters, Eastbourne, Sussex
Manufactured in Hong Kong by Regent Publishing Services Ltd
Printed in Hong Kong by Paramount Printing Co. Ltd.

Contents

Introduction to Art

Every time you paint or draw, you say something about yourself. It doesn't matter if you are painting an apple or the family dog, *you* will paint them as *you* see them. No one else will paint them quite like you do. And that's important. That's what art is about — showing people how you see things. You may draw from your imagination or dreams, but everyday objects — a teacup or a view through your window — are just as important.

In this book we show you different ways to paint and draw — with watercolor, tempera paints, colored pens, and pencils. All the artist's tools used are inexpensive and can be found in good stationers or artist's supply stores. We look at exciting, fun ways to use these tools — sponging on paint or blowing it with a straw.

Along the way we also help you turn yourself into a "real" artist, with tips on everything from mixing colors to using perspective. You may have thought of such skills as too hard, but we will show you how easy they can be. We suggest projects that give you the opportunity to practice your new skills, too. You will find that, with the help of this book, you'll soon start to paint pictures that you can be proud of.

Get Set

You have the ability to be an artist. In your paintings and drawings you can do what you want and express yourself freely. Sometimes your painting doesn't work. Sometimes it turns out better than you expected. By trying out all the different pencils, pens, and paints, you will find out what they can do. But first of all you need somewhere to paint.

Clean Water

You will have discovered that if the water you dip your brush into is dirty, your painting will be dirty. So, clean your brush well between colors and change your water as often as possible. When you have rinsed and dried your brushes, store them upside down in a dry jar.

Space to Create

You can be an artist at your desk, at a table, or on your lap. Find something hard to put your paper on. If you do not have a table, use a board. Have all your equipment – pens, pencils, paints, water jars – next to you, where you can reach them easily without stretching across your paper. Artists work better in a good light – from a window or a lamp.

Mixing Colors

This white plastic palette makes mixing colors easy, but an ordinary plate will do as well.

Paper Stretching

Have you noticed that watery paint sometimes makes the paper buckle and curl? You can stop this from happening to good quality paper by stretching it with water before you paint on it.

1 Lay the paper on a board and measure out four strips of brown gummed paper tape, one for each side.

2 With a clean, damp sponge, wet the surface of the paper and carefully flatten it on the board. Stick it down with the gummed strips along each edge. Allow it to dry. Now you have a piece of buckle-free paper.

Cheap, white paper is best for practicing drawing, but it will buckle when you paint.

Which Paper?

In an art or stationery store you will find lots of different kinds of paper – thick, thin, smooth, rough, tinted, white. They all feel different to draw and paint on. Thin, cheap paper is fine for practicing to draw, but you will find white drawing paper better for painting.

Look at the different papers here and see how they change the appearance of the orange paint stroke and the blue pastel mark we have tried out on each sheet. The cheap paper drinks up the paint so that the paint stroke loses its color. Compare it with the darker color and interesting "edge" of the paintmark on the special watercolor paper. The pastel mark is broken up by the rough pastel paper.

Special watercolor paper for wet techniques is expensive but is worth it for good results.

Tinted pastel paper is rougher on one side than the other.

Standard drawing paper from a sketch pad comes in different weights. You may need to stretch it (see this page) for watercolor.

Rough drawing paper will give your paint and pencil marks a textured effect.

Choosing Paints and Brushes

Paints that you mix with water – watercolors, tempera paints, and acrylics – are the easiest to use. They need not cost much to start with, although as you improve you may want to try more expensive paints that will have better, stronger colors. Oil paints are harder for the beginning artist to use well. They have not been included in this book.

▼ Going Halves (1)
In this windsurfing scene, you can see the effects of delicate water-color (top half). Tempera paints (used in bottom half), sometimes called poster paints, are bolder and thicker.

▼ Tempera and Gouache
These paints are thicker and more pasty than watercolors. You will find that the more water you add, the lighter a color gets. They dry lighter still.

▼ Pans of Color
Watercolors come in dry blocks or "pans." Unlike tempera paints, they are delicate colors, and are best used with lots of water. You will find they dry lighter than they look at first, but you can always darken them by painting on another layer once the first one is dry.

French ultramarine

Viridian

Cadmium red

Alizarin crimson

▼ Tubes of Color
Watercolor, gouache, and acrylic paints can be bought in tubes. Begin with a selection of ten "starter" colors like these. Then add to your collection as you become more experienced.

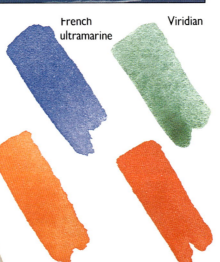

▶ Which Brush?

Brushes come in different sizes and shapes. The most common are "flat," which are square, or "round," which are shaped like a teardrop. They are made of anything from nylon "hair" to hog bristle. You can tell the size of a brush by its number. No. 16 is the biggest, and No. 000 the smallest.

A large, flat brush useful for flat washes (see below).

A large, round brush for broad areas of color.

Use a small brush for touches of color or highlights.

A No. 5 round brush is the best one to start with.

A Wash of Color

When you begin a painting, it is usually best to start with the background color – the sky, or maybe a beach. Then, when this pale, watery wash is dry, you can paint your flowers, trees, or hills on top. You can paint a wash with watercolor, acrylics, or tempera paints.

1 Mix a lot of water and very little paint in a small dish. Load your brush and, starting at the top, move the brush evenly across the paper, from side to side.

2 You will find that a ridge of color collects along the base of each stroke. Brush it away with the next stroke, moving the color smoothly to the edge. Aim for an even wash of color.

Yellow ocher

Raw umber

Payne's gray

▶ Acrylics

Acrylics come in rich, glossy colors which cover the paper easily. They can be watered down and used like watercolors, or used thickly straight from the jar or tube. Wash dirty brushes in water.

Lemon yellow

Cadmium yellow

Cerulean blue

Soft 4B pencil

Standard HB pencil

Blackboard chalk

Chalk pastel

Oil pastel

Colored pencil

Hard wax crayon

Water-soluble colored pencil

Water-soluble crayon

Pencils, Crayons, and Pastels

Try painting and drawing with any colors you can lay your hands on. Pencils, crayons, and pastels all have different uses. Colored pencils are hard and dry, and travel well in pencil cases. You will find some new ways to use them on this page. Crayons are not just for toddlers. For a start, they combine well with paints for some fun effects (see pages 32–33). Pastels can be chalky or oily. Blend them with your fingers or use them like pencils.

Top Marks

The look of your picture will depend on the type of pencil or crayon you use. By trying them out, you can see what suits you best. Here we show you how different the marks can be.

Just Add Water

Some pencils and crayons can be used dry or wet. Water blends or spreads the color as in paint. You can either apply a wet brush to marks you have made on the paper, or dip the crayon in water and then draw with it. Experiment by copying the color triangle on pages 24–25 using both pencils and crayons. You will soon see how different they are.

Mixing Exercises

As with paints, you can mix dry colors to create different colors or hues. But if you cannot mix them with water like paints, you have to use other ways such as overlapping layers, or mixing dots of color, as shown opposite. With pastels you can mix by gently blending colors together with your finger. Use these ideas for shading effects.

Color Mixing

You can mix dry color by dotting colors side by side. When you look at the dots from a distance, your eyes will do the mixing for you. Dots of red and yellow will appear as orange, or blue and yellow as green.

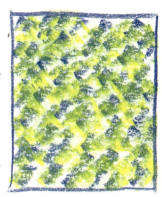

Shading

With pencils you can make dark or light shading just by pressing harder or softer. Practice this shading technique with free, sweeping strokes. Start by pressing hard, then letting the stroke get softer.

Crosshatching

These crisscross lines are useful for shading. When you are cross-hatching like this, try using two colors so that you are mixing the color at the same time.

Going Halves (2)

See how chalk and oil pastels can make your picture look quite different. Oil pastels (above) make a strong mark. Chalk pastels (below) are drier and softer. Try both to see which you like better.

1 Try mixing pencil, crayon, or pastel by overlapping one color with another. Here we begin with a purple pencil, starting dark and getting lighter.

2 Now add the second color, overlapping the first one to start with. Start light and get darker. Where the two colors combine, a third color appears.

To mix pastels, shade two blocks of color side by side. Now rub your finger gently across the blocks to form a third.

17

A fine tip for line drawing.

A broad felt-tip to fill in areas of color.

A water-soluble pen with brush tip.

The type of useful, multi-purpose pen you find in a set.

A trusty ballpoint for all types of drawing.

Picking Pens

Felt-tip and stylist pens are cheap to buy, bright in color, and easy to use. If you are designing something to catch the eye – a poster or a birthday card – then these pens are the answer. You can buy inexpensive sets with standard-sized tips in a good range of colors. It is also useful to have some thin-tipped pens for linework, and some thicker ones for filling in areas of color.

Overlapping Colors

The ink in many types of felt-tips is transparent. This means you can apply one color over another to create more colors. Experiment with your colors and see what unexpected hues you can produce.

Mixing Pens

You will find that you can make some interesting effects by mixing colors with your felt-tip and stylist pens. Once the marks have been made, water-based inks can be mixed on the page with a wet brush. However, they will take a while to dry. Permanent inks dry almost immediately and do not run together so easily; they are better for crosshatching.

Yellow over blue

Red over blue

Yellow and blue over red

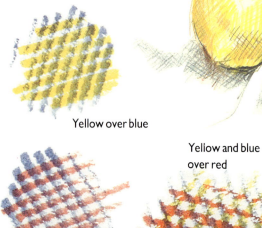

Crossed Lines

By crosshatching lines of different colors, you will create the illusion of a new color. Look how this has been used in the drawing of fruit above.

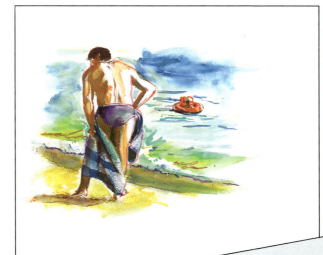

◀ Felt-Tip Fun
Look how clever you can be with felt-tip pens. Water has been painted on to make shadows and to color the sea. Old, nearly dry, pens are useful for textured effects, as on the towel.

▶ Pen Friends
Ballpoint pens are fun to sketch with and they are easy to carry around. They produce a good smooth line that you can make darker or lighter by pressing harder or softer. Take care to start at the top of the page and work down or you may smudge the ink.

Spots Before the Eyes

By dotting and spotting colors together, you can create a whole range of colors and textures. This technique is called pointillism and can be done well with felt-tips.

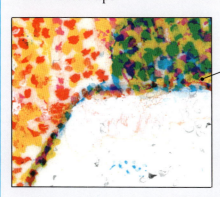

Looking at Shape

We recognize things by their shape. But sometimes this shape can seem too complicated to draw. One way to tackle this problem is to "fit" a difficult shape into a simple one, as shown below. Remember that an object changes its shape depending on the angle from which you look at it. As a new artist, you must learn to see the shape in front of you as it really is, not as you expect it to be.

Changing Shape

You have to think hard when you are copying a shape because it changes as you move around it. Keep looking up at the object and back to your paper to check that you have it right.

Circle
To draw any object that is basically a circular shape, such as an apple, draw a circle first. Then see how the outline of the object differs from the circle. This should make it easier to draw.

Square
You may think a cushion is square, but it will never be quite regular. Use the square to guide you, but notice how the outline of the cushion bursts out of the square or doesn't quite touch its edges.

Rectangle
A rectangle can be the basis for a car, a house, or a loaf of bread.

Triangle
By drawing a triangle first, you will find it easier to make a pitcher symmetrical.

20

Cup Watch

Seen from above, the rim of the cup is a circle, but it doesn't look much like a cup! Viewed from the side, the cup's rim becomes an ellipse, or squashed circle. Now you can recognize it!

Tricky Tire

Look how the shape of the tire changes from different angles. From the side it is round, but from everywhere else, it is an ellipse. Draw a truck from various viewpoints (far left) to practice this.

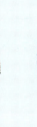

Easier Than It Looks

This test will show how you can train yourself to look at shapes and outlines. Study the small picture above but, with a pencil, copy the upside-down illustration (right). Turned upside down, the girl's face becomes simply a pattern of lines that is easier to copy.

21

Toning Up

A pencil can make light or dark marks on paper. Artists say that these marks vary in tone, or tonal value. In these three strips, the tone varies from dark at the top to light at the bottom. With a pencil (left and center), you reduce the tone by pressing less hard. In the paint strip (right) the tone is reduced by adding white.

Light and Shade

We do not need to feel something to know its shape. An apple is round, a box is square. We understand their form without touching them because we can see shadows curve around the apple, while the shadow falls straight down on the box. Artists say that light and shade "model" the shape. If you want your painting or drawing to look real on a flat page, you need to use shadows and highlights to show the shapes of the objects and make them three-dimensional.

Model Shadows

Light models, or gives shape to, objects. Highlights are created where the light falls, while surfaces hidden from the light are cast into shadow.

Light

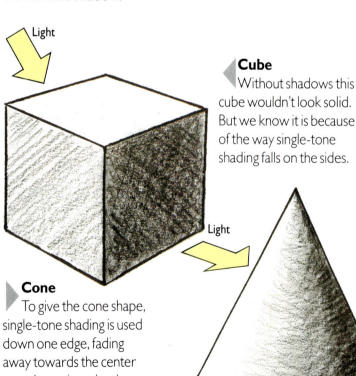

Cube
Without shadows this cube wouldn't look solid. But we know it is because of the way single-tone shading falls on the sides.

Light

Cone
To give the cone shape, single-tone shading is used down one edge, fading away towards the center to make a triangular shape.

Light

Cylinder
The shading down one edge of the cylinder fades away as it rounds the curve. This makes the object appear solid.

Sphere
This is the most difficult shape to model. The shading fades away towards the center to make a crescent shape.

Light

Seeing the Light

Always look carefully to see where the light is coming from – the light source. Remember to add the highlights on the side where the light first touches the object, and shade the side farthest from the light source (see right). Cast shadows are affected by the direction and angle of the light source: (1) high light source from left; (2) low light source from behind.

Wrong
Look again. The light strikes the pepper grinder from the right. So that is where the highlights should be.

Right
Now it's right. Here the highlights are brightest where the object is closest to the light source.

Shaping with Color

You have seen that light and shade can be used to make objects appear solid. Color can be used to do this, too, as this drawing of an apple shows.

1 With a circle as your basic shape, use a pencil to draw the outline of an apple.

2 Fill in the basic colors, leaving white areas for the highlights, to suggest shine.

3 With a darker color, shade the apple, fading gently into the center. Finally, add the shadow cast by the apple on the ground.

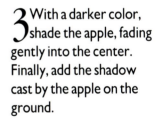

Looking at Color

Clever use of color can add interest to any painting. As a new artist, you need to understand how to mix three colors – red, blue, and yellow – to make almost any other color you can think of. Because all the others are made from them, these three are called primary colors. You also need to learn how to really see the color in a scene – the sea is not always blue or the grass green – so that you are able to paint it well.

Getting Lighter
Different media are "lightened" in different ways. Watercolor (far left) becomes lighter as you add more water. Gouache (center) can be made paler with water or white paint. With a pencil (left), the tone gets lighter the less you press.

Color Surprises
You need not add black to darken a color. In fact, black often just makes a color dull. Yellow can be darkened by adding just a touch of purple, green by adding a dash of red, orange by adding a dash of blue.

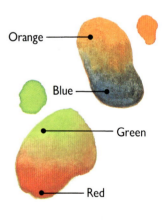

Orange
Blue
Green
Red

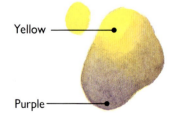

Yellow
Purple

Yellow
Orange
Red
Green
Purple
Blue

Take Three Colors
Try to copy this triangle. It will help you to understand how to mix colors. On a palette, start with a blob of yellow. Then add red, a little at a time. (You should always add a darker color to a lighter one.) The color will change through orange to red. Now start again with a second blob of yellow and add blue. Finally, start with a blob of red and add blue.

Black-and-White Vision

If we look at a black-and-white photograph of a painting, we can judge the tonal values of the colors used – just how "black" or "white" they are. Bright summer sun, as in this scene, makes dark shadows and bright highlights. Try painting an object – a pitcher say – with mixes of only black and white.

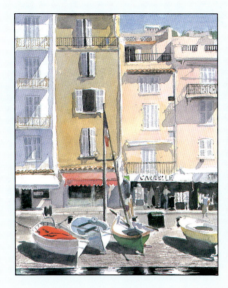

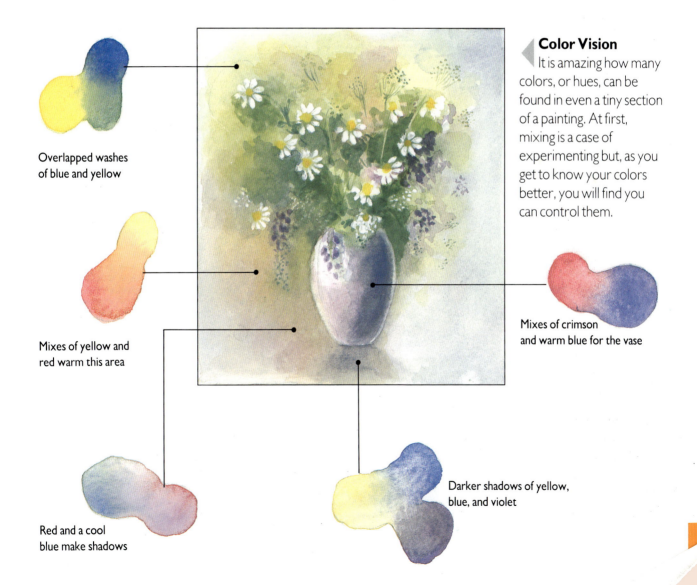

Overlapped washes of blue and yellow

Mixes of yellow and red warm this area

Red and a cool blue make shadows

Color Vision

It is amazing how many colors, or hues, can be found in even a tiny section of a painting. At first, mixing is a case of experimenting but, as you get to know your colors better, you will find you can control them.

Mixes of crimson and warm blue for the vase

Darker shadows of yellow, blue, and violet

Composing your Picture

You are searching for a view to sketch. Everything seems big, crowded, and messy. So, look for a small corner of the scene. Find one that has less in it but some unusual shapes, different lines, colors, and textures. What you are doing is arranging your view. You can choose what you want to include and the angle you view it from – high up or low down. The final arrangement is called your composition.

Simple Sketches
In your sketchbook (see page 28), try out lots of different views of the same scene. They need only be small, such as the ones shown here.

This little boat with its tall mast begs to be framed in the portrait shape.

Again, the vertical masts and houses look better in this portrait frame.

Messy View
A jumble of boats, this harbor view is a mess. Where should you start? The solution is to walk around your subject a bit. Find a detail, in this case maybe a single boat, and view it from different angles until you find a happy balance of form and space.

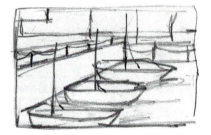

Viewed from an angle, this row of boats invites you deep into the picture.

A landscape frame suits this panoramic view of the sea.

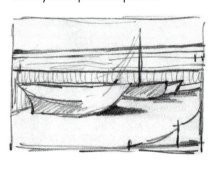

The main lines here are horizontal, from side to side. So a landscape frame is the obvious choice.

Shaping Up
When you sketch a scene, you can choose to make it a "landscape" shape, which is wider than it is tall, (above and left), or "portrait" which is taller than it is wide, like those at the top. You will find it makes a difference to the balance of the composition.

Framing the View

A viewfinder is an excellent device used by artists. It is a type of portable frame you can carry with your sketchbook. If you look through it, you frame the scene and see how it would look on your page. You can also try out landscape and portrait shapes and see which looks better.

▲ Final Choice
This was the artist's final choice for the composition. Would you have chosen it? Can you see how the artist walked around the harbor view in the muddled photograph on the opposite page and focused on this boat, framing it with the water behind?

▲ To make your own viewfinder, take a piece of paper or cardboard 6 × 7 inches (15 × 18 cm) and cut out a rectangle 4 × 5 inches (10 × 13 cm) from the center. Two L-shaped pieces of cardboard can be even more useful. They can be held as shown above, and the size of the frame adjusted to suit you. Try it out around the room. Doesn't the world look different?

27

Inexpensive, ring-bound sketchbook

Ring-bound, pastel-paper pad

Small, rough-surfaced pad

Hardback, bound sketchbook

Keeping a Sketchbook

A sketchbook is fun to keep. If you carry one around with you and use it all the time, you will find it becomes more like a diary. It is where notes, ideas, and information are stored – faces, places, a funny dog, an interesting door. When you sit down to paint, you can remind yourself of the things you have seen to jump-start your imagination.

◀ Which Sketchbook?

You may like to have a ring-bound sketchbook as they are easier to fold back. One with a hard cover is useful when you cannot find a surface to support your work. It doesn't need to be huge – a pocket-sized one is fine.

▼ Just Testing

Test out techniques and different paints, pencils, and crayons in your sketchbook. Then when you want to produce a particular effect, you can look back at these pages.

Enlarging

When you want to use a small sketch as the basis for a large drawing or painting, you may find it difficult to copy your sketch in a larger size. By enlarging it by grid, as shown here, you copy one square at a time so that you keep your picture in proportion.

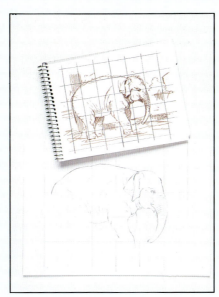

With a ruler, carefully measure and draw a grid of regularly-spaced squares over your sketch. Now, on your drawing paper, draw a similar grid with the same number of squares, but make it as big as you need – twice or three times the original size. Next, copy your sketch, square by square.

When, say, you are copying the line of the elephant's trunk, mark where it crosses the edge of a square. Pencil it in with the same flow as the original.

Try It Out
Draw freely. Try to grasp the shape and outline to start with. Don't tear up your "mistakes," they can give you ideas later on. Try taking a sketch across two pages.

Odds and Ends
Your sketchbook can also be a scrapbook full of ideas and images. Paste postcards, magazine pictures, photographs, among your own drawings to build a busy artist's reference book.

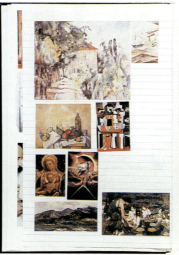

At Home

Once you discover the different characters of your pencils, pens, and paints, you will need something to copy – a subject. You do not need to go farther than your own home. Look around you. Your bedroom should be a good place to start. How about drawing the rumpled shirt on the floor of your room, or maybe the neatly folded one on your chair? Furniture and covers can make good subjects and backgrounds as you will see. Chairs and tables can be arranged simply, but look for an original viewpoint. Or you can paint a portrait of your favorite stuffed toy on the bed.

What about the kitchen? There are so many odd-looking gadgets to study here, not to mention fresh food in the refrigerator and packets and cans in the cupboards. Everyone draws apples, so make yours more interesting by taking a bite out of it or cutting it in half.

Then, of course, you may be able to persuade your family pets, or even your family, to pose. If not, try and catch them when they are asleep! We will be looking closely at people and the way they move, and giving you tips about painting portraits. And to help you with your pets, we'll look at ways of painting fur, feathers, and scales.

Keep your sketchbook at hand so that you can record everything around you. This will give you a ready store of ideas and images.

Blot for a Bloom

Certain fruit, like grapes and plums, have a white powder on their skins called a bloom. You can give grapes a bloom with a tissue.

1 First paint in the grape color – here, purple and green allowed to run into each other.

2 Now, wind tissue around your index finger. Blot up spots of surface paint, leaving the stained paper to form a soft bloom.

Food for Art

O nce you start looking for things to draw and paint, you will stop thinking of fruit and vegetables as food and start seeing them in terms of form, color, and texture – lumpy, bumpy cauliflowers, smooth, shiny tomatoes, curly lettuces. There are lots of artist's tricks to help you capture these wonderful forms and textures.

Apple Colors
The secret of this watercolor study is that the artist has built up the color with layers of paint: first a wash of pale yellow, followed, when dry, by curving strokes of green and red, and then white gouache highlights.

Grape Variety
The artist has really looked at these grapes. No two grapes are exactly the same shape or color. Note the bloom.

Wax Works

Because wax repels, or resists, water, if you paint watercolor over wax stripes, it only stays on the areas of paper without wax. This technique is called "wax resist," and can be used to produce some interesting effects, as we show you here. You can use a candle for the wax, or wax crayons if you want the color to show.

Waxy Orange

The highlight on the rough skin of this orange is the white of the paper showing through the watercolor wash. The trick here is that textured, grainy paper was used, combined with the wax resist method described below.

Mixed Fruit

Before starting this fruit bowl in colored pencil, the artist took time to study the detail – first the fruit colors, then the shapes.

1 Draw the shape of a squash very lightly with a pencil. Now, "draw" in the pale stripes of the squash skin with a white wax candle.

2 Mix a watery yellow with clean water. With a big, soft brush, wash the yellow over the whole squash shape. Do you see how the wax resists the paint?

3 Let the yellow dry. Now make wax stripes over the yellow with the candle. Mix watery green and wash this over the squash shape to finish your work.

33

Everyday Objects

Look around you and you will find lots of objects to paint and draw – pencils in a jar, an earthenware pitcher, or a bunch of keys. These household objects have interesting shapes and surfaces that can test your skills as an artist. A painting or drawing of such non-living objects is called a still life.

▼ Watering Can
Poster paints are good for hard, shiny surfaces. Paint dark shadows over a lighter base color, then add white highlights.

▲ Keys
The skill here is in the drawing of these complicated shapes. Watercolor has been added carefully, almost as an afterthought.

▲ Bottle
Glass is always a challenge. Try using pastels, which are easy to control when creating the reflections.

Working Sight Size

You will find it easier if you copy things the same size as you see them. This is called working sight size. It means you may have to go closer to what you want to draw to fill your page, or farther away if it doesn't fit on the page. Move until you see the objects at the right size for your paper.

▲ Candle
Oil pastels are well suited to the smooth texture of this candle. The surface is built up by working one color into another.

Arranging a Still Life

Objects from around the house make a good still life. Make several sketches before deciding on the final arrangement.

▼ This is one view of these household objects. The arrangement is rather unnatural.

▶ Now the pot is full of dark-brown coffee, changing the balance of the composition.

▼ After sketching a number of views and arrangements the artist chose this composition for a detailed still life in tempera paints.

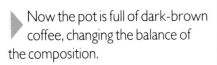

▼ Try moving the objects around a bit. By coming closer in, the reflections on the pot become important.

Painting Glass

Glass reflects colors and distorts shapes seen through it. You will find it easier to paint a glass if you look at it as a jigsaw of colored shapes.

1 Make an outline drawing in pencil, mapping out the colored shapes in the glass. Wash in the background colors. Then start on the paler areas of color.

2 Look at the shapes of the gray shadows and paint them in. Now add highlights in white, painting along a ruler for straight lines.

3 There are stronger shadows where the glass thickens at its base. Add little touches of dark gray here to increase the contrasts between light and dark.

35

Focus on Furniture

Furniture is practical. You use it every day. You sit on chairs, eat or work at a table, and sleep in a bed. So, it's easy to overlook the fact that furniture is also beautiful, intricate, even ugly. As you explore your home with sketchbook in hand, look at the furniture. You will be amazed by the interesting shapes and colors you will find.

▼ Sofa Shapes
Move the chair around and look for some unusual viewpoints. Here you can see the sofa through the back of the chair. Breaking up the sofa like this makes you look at it in a different way.

▲ New View
When you use a camera, you find yourself forced to see things in a new way. Soft, curved lines form the sofa arm. Harder lines are used for the wooden chair.

▶ Hard and Soft
Look at the shapes made by the curves and angles, but also capture the softness of the sofa in contrast to the hard chair.

Folding Fabrics

When sketching a room, you will probably find yourself drawing folding fabrics – curtains, a shawl over a chair or bed covers. Try not to see folds as straight lines on the material; look at each fold as a shape. Curtains will change depending on whether the light is shining on or through them. Try a tonal sketch (see pages 24–25) of a curtain to explore this.

1 Pencil in the outline of the curtain and the shapes of the folds. Paint in the background and shadow areas, leaving the highlights as white paper.

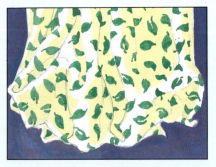

2 Once dry, apply the pattern across the folds, making sure that parts of it curve around the folds and "disappear" behind them.

Cutting In

Cutting the chair and sofa with the frame makes an almost abstract picture of shapes and spaces, rather than of a sofa and chair.

Camera Angles

You are so familiar with your own bedroom, it may be difficult to see anything interesting to draw. Use your camera and take photos from a variety of angles. Perhaps you might choose to focus on the angled view above.

Artist's Choice

The artist chose this arrangement of stuffed toys to set off the bedroom furniture. The different textures are captured with colored pencils.

3 Now add the shadows. Then, with a fine brush, outline the deepest folds with black. Add white highlights to the outer folds where the light falls.

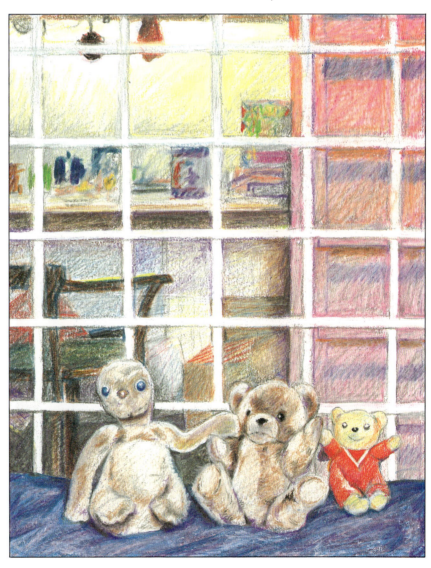

Project: Still Life

These peppers and eggplant, which you might find in your kitchen, make a good still life. Peppers are colored so brightly, with shiny skins and unexpected forms. Eggplants are smoother, almost silky to touch. Surrounded by a softer fabric bag, these textures become the main challenge.

Think about your composition and take time to arrange the vegetables. Consider the source of light as this will affect the arrangement you choose. It may be from a lamp overhead or natural light from a window. For this project, felt-tip markers were used, including watercolor markers.

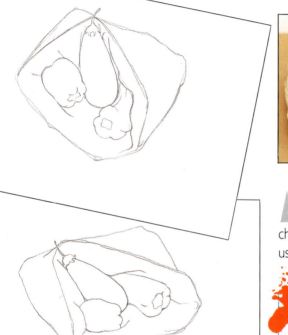

▲ **Quick Snapshot**
A photograph of your chosen arrangement can be a useful reference.

1 When you have decided the still life is right, make a more detailed sketch and draw in the outlines with fine felt-tip markers.

▲ **Quick Sketches**
Prepare by making some sketches to explore your arrangement. Try out different viewpoints, from above or with your nose level with the table.

Test Strip

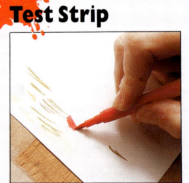

It is sometimes difficult to tell how colors or mixes will look on your paper. Keep a corner of your sheet for testing them.

2 Now add a foundation wash with watercolor markers. First make a few marks on the paper. Then dip your finger in water and smooth out the color.

3 After looking carefully at your still life, use the markers without water to build up strong areas of color. Leave the highlights as the washed paper showing through.

4 Next add the finer details of the stalks and shadows. Note how the background cloth has been built up with overlaid hatching in different colors.

5 The frayed tip of this damaged marker was useful to draw the stalk of the eggplant.

▼ **Texture Contrasts**
What a success! The artist has captured the shiny textures of the vegetables and contrasted them with the soft fabric bag.

People Shapes

The trick with drawing people is to look at them as objects. Forget that you are sketching your sister or your grandmother. Just think of them as shape and form. People shapes are fascinating because they are always changing, always new. A sitting body takes on a new form when it stands; a squatting body is different from a sleeping body. Sketch your family as they move around the house.

Slumped Figure
Sketch a person slumped in a comfortable chair. Observe the long sloping line of the back, and the sharp angles of the knees.

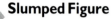

Rectangular Pose
This person shape fits into a simple rectangle. Knees, elbows, and feet make precise angles.

Relative Sizes

When you are drawing a person it helps if you remember that the various parts of the body relate to each other, that the human body has standard proportions. As you can see in these drawings, in the adult man, the distance from neck to feet is six times the size of the head. But the proportions are different for the girl (head 1, rest of body 5) and the toddler (head 1, rest of body 3). You can use these standard proportions to help you with lengths of arms and legs, too.

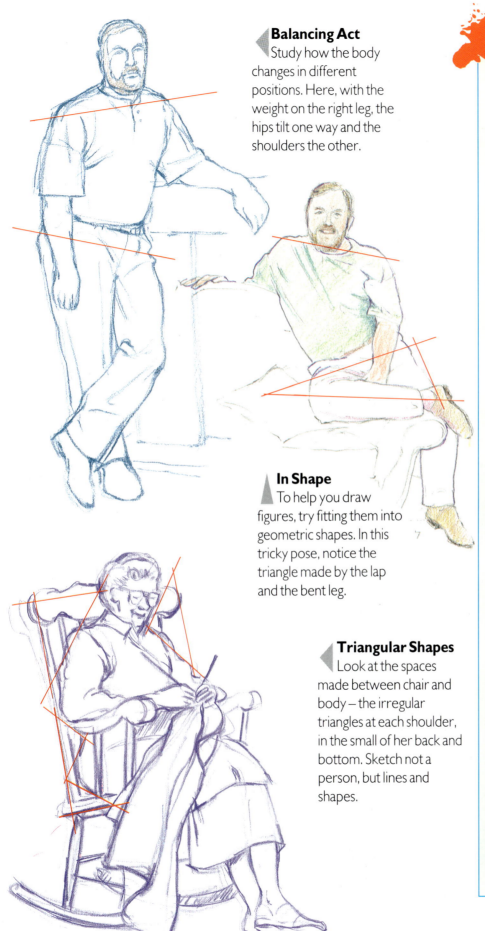

Balancing Act
Study how the body changes in different positions. Here, with the weight on the right leg, the hips tilt one way and the shoulders the other.

In Shape
To help you draw figures, try fitting them into geometric shapes. In this tricky pose, notice the triangle made by the lap and the bent leg.

Triangular Shapes
Look at the spaces made between chair and body – the irregular triangles at each shoulder, in the small of her back and bottom. Sketch not a person, but lines and shapes.

A Quick Measure

You might like to draw your figure within grid lines, as shown in the box on the opposite page. But as a quick guide to check that the body proportions are right, you can always use the top of your pencil.

Hold your arm out straight in front of you with the pencil upright in your hand. Align the top of the pencil with the top of the person's head, and put your thumbnail on the pencil level with the person's chin. Keeping your thumb in place, move the pencil down the body to see how many times the length of the head goes into the length of the body.

Moving Figures

Stick Shapes
Sketching people as stickmen will help you grasp the basic lines of a moving body.

Observe the line of the spine. Here it is a sharp curve.

Reaching up, the body is almost in a straight line. But notice the arch in the spine.

The parts of the body have a natural sense of balance. If the hips jut forwards, the shoulders go back.

The body changes shape very clearly when a person is crawling.

As an artist, you will develop a quick hand and a sharp eye so that you can capture movement. Do not worry about details of the body you are sketching, but look at the shape it makes as it bends, leaps, stretches, and crawls. You will begin to see how bodies shift their weight and hold their balance, the position of the shoulders in relation to the feet, or the angles of the hips and knees.

Basic Shapes
Train your eye to see the basic shape of a figure. This will help you catch the pose before the person moves. If you notice that these bending figures form triangles, your hand will quickly record the lines that the body makes within that shape.

Clothes in Action

The folds in people's clothing play an important part in creating a sense of movement in their bodies.

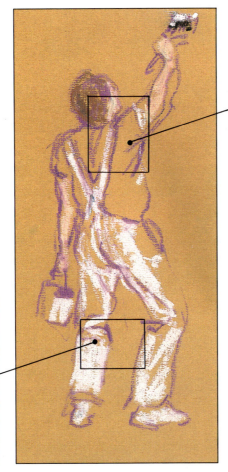

Moving Parts
The fluid pastel strokes used to show the play of light and shadow over these folds help to express the movement in this drawing.

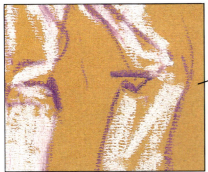

Material Differences
Fabric imitates body movements. Some materials are thin and clingy, following every line of the body's form, such as in this T-shirt. Others, such as in this painter's overalls, are loose and bulky, creating heavy folds where the body bends and twists.

Body Lines
Notice how people place their arms and imagine the line of the spine. The tilt of the head and the slope of the shoulder are very important, too.

Right Lines
Here you can see how the artist has explored the line with his ball-point pen. He would have looked up at the figure and back at the paper again and again, drawing several soft lines for, say, the stomach before firming up the one that felt right.

When you draw a face laughing or crying, certain lines change shape. We all know that the mouth turns up when we smile, but eyes change shape, too.

Smile Lines
A smile forces the cheeks up against the eyes making them crescent-shaped.

Angry Looks
In anger, the mouth is small and straight and the brow furrows.

Down in the Mouth
An unhappy face has a wide, downward-sloping mouth and tilted eyebrows.

Making Faces

You can sketch a head and how it tilts and turns and then, with a few lines, fill in the eyes, nose, and mouth to make a "face." But to draw a face you know, your mother's, father's, or best friend's, you need to observe carefully and record details. Are the eyes close together? What shape is the mouth? If you manage this, your face then becomes a portrait.

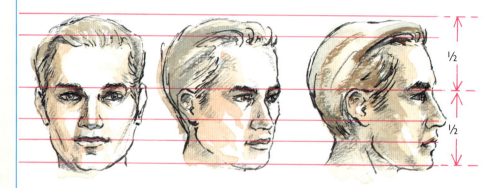

Head Lines
Like the body, the face has standard proportions. Notice how the forehead, nose, and chin fit into the head. You may well be surprised to find that the eyes come halfway down, and to see how close the mouth is to the chin line. Of course, as the head turns, these proportions stay the same.

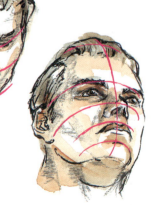

Different Angles
The proportions of the face change when seen at an angle from above or below. In the upturned face, the distance between the mouth and chin is exaggerated and the forehead appears shorter. The features of the downturned head run into each other, and the forehead seems overly large.

Flesh Tones

Skin is not simply "black" or "white," but many colors and tones in between. Everyone's skin is slightly different. Here, these flesh tints have been mixed in gouache from variations of the primary colors, plus white. But only a *touch* of each color has been used.

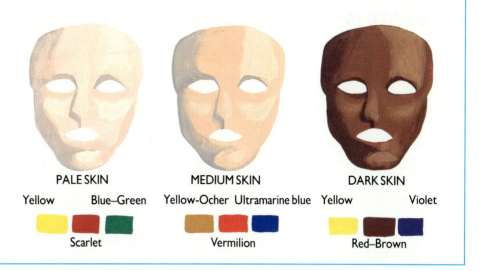

PALE SKIN

Yellow   Blue–Green

Scarlet

MEDIUM SKIN

Yellow-Ocher   Ultramarine blue

Vermilion

DARK SKIN

Yellow   Violet

Red–Brown

▲ Look Again

This is a good try, but can you see how the flesh is a bit flat and pink. The artist has not noticed how the skin has shadows and highlights – around the eyes, along the jawline, around the mouth.

▲ Well Done

Here the flesh tones are more subtle. The artist has used touches of violet and green for the shadows, and yellow and white for the highlights. Daring mixing captures the shape of the face.

45

Project: Myself

This project is about you. There is no better subject because you are always conveniently around, ready to pose. In this project, too, we will look more closely at how to use watercolor. It is a good medium for a portrait because it is a delicate, transparent paint that suits skin tones and textures. Now, what are you going to wear? Put on something that expresses your character – perhaps a favorite hat or T-shirt.

Mirror Image
Position yourself close enough to the mirror to be able to see yourself clearly, but leave enough space on your work table to lay out your paints and brushes.

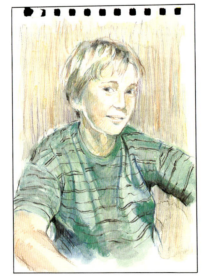

Getting It Right
Before you start the portrait itself, try out different poses and outfits in the mirror and then do some color sketches. You can then see what works best. The artist has chosen to do these sketches in colored pencil and watercolor wash.

1 Once you have chosen the pose you like best, pencil in your outline and main details. Mark in the highlights to remind yourself to leave them unpainted. With a thick brush and watery paint, wash in the skin, hair, T-shirt, and background, painting around the highlights.

2 Once the first wash is dry, look for the shadows on your face, hair, and clothes. Now, add another layer of color to these areas. Use the same colors as in step 1, but with less water. You may need to apply several layers, allowing each one to dry.

3 You are gradually building up the layers of paint over the shadow areas. The highlights are the white paper, the light parts, the thin wash, the mid-shadows, more layers. Now work on the darker areas of shadow. With a fine brush, add details.

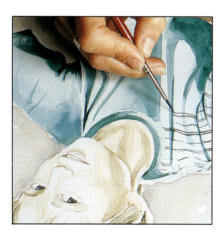

4 Add more detail with a finely pointed brush, as the artist is doing with the T-shirt stripes here. Relax your hand and don't worry if the line is not even – it won't be over the folds of clothes.

▶ **Spitting Image**
To finish, add touches of brownish red to the lips, the corners of the eyes, the ear, and to the hair. It looks good.

Animal Art

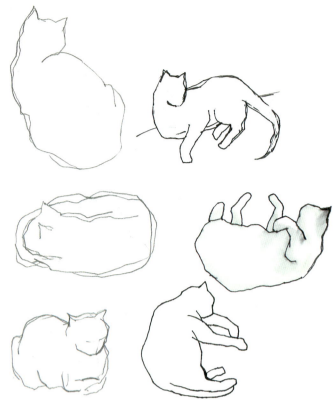

Pets are good subjects to draw around the home because they are always there! Study them carefully when they are asleep and get to know their shapes. Animals often walk off or change position when you are drawing, so you will need to work fast. They are also quite tricky to draw accurately, but don't let this stop you from trying. Remember, no drawing is wrong, but part of your way of learning to express your own talent.

◀ **Pet Photograph**
Your pet will not listen when you beg it to sit still while you sketch. Photographs will help you to study poses. Why not try drawing this mischievous cat.

▼ **Sleeping Sketches**
Whip out your sketchbook as your cat settles down to sleep. Move around your subject to sketch it from various angles. Use pencil or a watercolor marker washed with water.

Animal Shapes

To keep the parts of your pet in proportion, try looking at it as a series of geometric shapes. For instance, many dogs – terriers or spaniels – fit into a horizontal rectangle, with the head and legs, and even ears and tail, as smaller rectangles. Seeing your pet in this way will help you decide the relative sizes of the different parts of its body.

◀ This rabbit is a series of ovals of different sizes, from the body, to the head and thigh, right to the tiny tail.

▼ Capture the rough shape of your rabbit with ovals. Then study it and see how the outline of your pet differs.

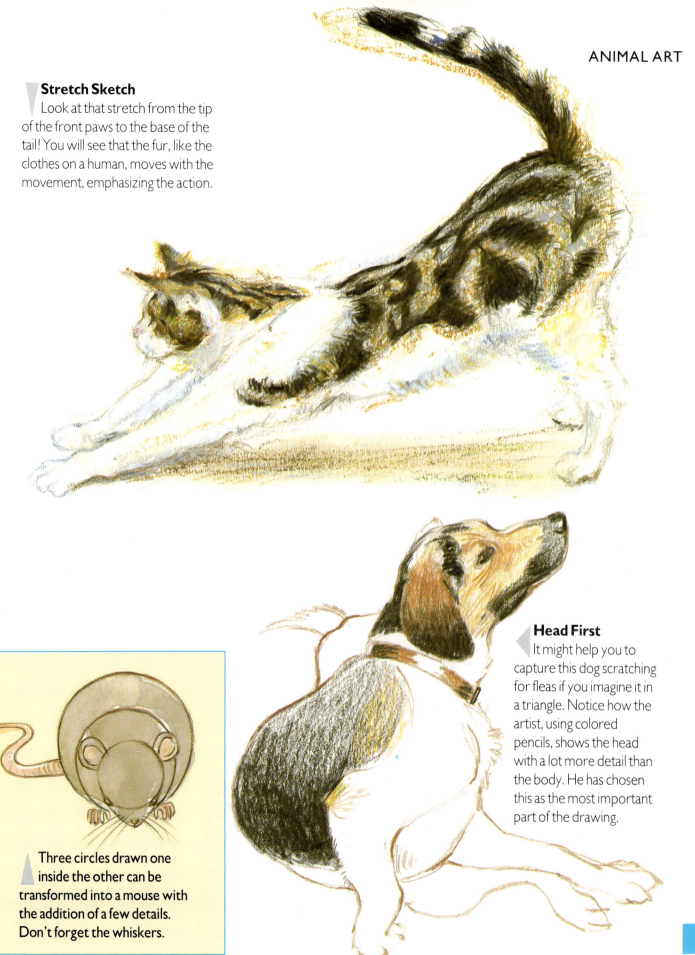

▼ Stretch Sketch
Look at that stretch from the tip of the front paws to the base of the tail! You will see that the fur, like the clothes on a human, moves with the movement, emphasizing the action.

◀ Head First
It might help you to capture this dog scratching for fleas if you imagine it in a triangle. Notice how the artist, using colored pencils, shows the head with a lot more detail than the body. He has chosen this as the most important part of the drawing.

▲ Three circles drawn one inside the other can be transformed into a mouse with the addition of a few details. Don't forget the whiskers.

Animal Hair and Fur

S ome animals, such as seals, have such short fur that drawing it is almost like drawing skin. Others are so furry that you can use all sorts of interesting techniques to portray the texture. Some media may seem easier to use for fur – pencils allow you to draw every hair. But you will find all media – paint, pastels, and crayons – have different advantages when you paint and draw animals.

A Dry Brush

With paint, you can copy the texture of fur very easily using the dry brush technique. Use thick paint, and not too much, so that the brush stays "dry." Different brushes will produce different types of "fur." Try them out.

◢ Dip your brush in the paint, then blot it fairly dry on tissue. Now, spread the bristles between thumb and finger as you drag the brush across the paper.

◢ **Rubbing Along**
When using colored pencil, you can use your eraser to create texture by rubbing out color to make highlights. Try dragging the eraser along pencil lines to soften them for long, fine hair. Lots of short, lively strokes create this bushy tail.

▼ Cat Coat
This cat's glossy, tortoiseshell coat was built up with layers of tempera paint, using the dry brush technique (see left).

Furry Effects

Using different media – watercolor, felt-tip, and oil pastels – brings out different characteristics in these three mouse portraits.

▲ With watercolor, the
glossy coat of the mouse is painted with the dry brush method shown on the opposite page.

▼ Fur Colors
With gouache and tempera paint you can paint light over dark. Use a fine brush to paint the hairs in individual strokes over the basic colors.

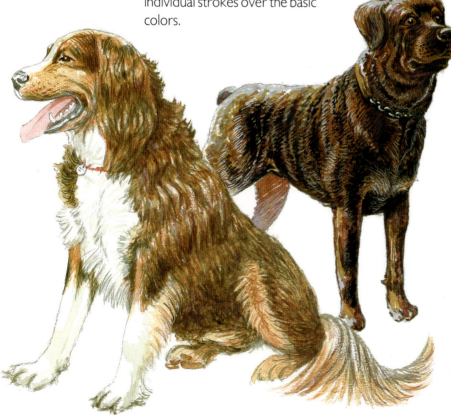

▲ The texture of the coat is
shown with short strokes of color using felt-tip markers.

▲ In oil pastels, the fur
highlights are scratched out with a needle.

Feathers and Scales

We are lucky to have such an extraordinary range of birds, reptiles, and fish to paint and draw. Feathers are beautiful, delicate forms that are good to sketch even on their own. But when you are drawing a bird, you don't have to paint in every one – nor every scale on a fish. The artist has to capture the texture and color of large masses of feathers or scales with a few strokes, seeking out the details that make a particular bird or fish special.

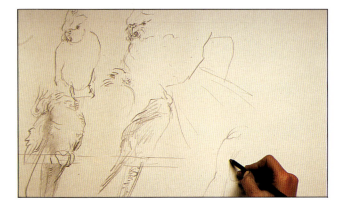

Quick on the Draw
Birds tend to be restless so make numerous, quick sketches. Don't worry about getting it "right" – just remember, the more sketches you make, the more confident you will become.

Bright Bird
With gouache, the intricate feather patterns on this parakeet are carefully marked. The white highlights give the feathers a texture you want to touch.

Goose Feathers
A stylist pen is used to color-sketch this goose. The impression of feathers is made with both the simple black outline and the flat gray shading in two tones.

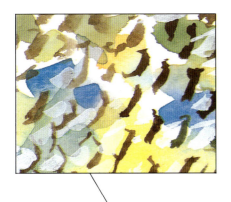

Scale Colors
Note the range of color and tone in the watercolor patchwork with added white paint highlights.

Lizard Line
An artist can use the outline of an animal to give a clue to the texture of its skin.

Color Polishing

You can "polish" your colors. The technique of burnishing is used with colored pencils.

1 Sketch the fish, then fill in with colored pencils. Now rub over these colors with a white pencil to polish them and make them shimmer.

2 You can add more color – use thick strokes. Polish this layer by rubbing it with a blunt knitting needle.

Neck Detail
Over delicate washes of blue and green, the scales were added with a fine brush and brown paint.

Fish Finish
In the finished portrait, the goldfish looks shiny. Burnishing is great for scales.

Scaly Snake
Dots of white paint form highlights over crosshatched colored pencil, giving a scaly sheen.

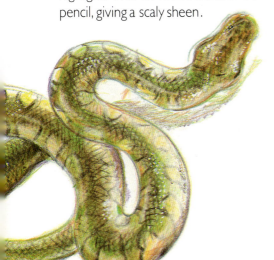

Project: My Pet

Making a portrait of your pet may sound easier than it is. As you have already found out, pets do not naturally stay still for very long. So get ready to do some quick sketches to capture the shape and position you want. Then you need to study your subject for color and details only. For example, you can always study the eye when you get to that detail, even if your pet has moved from its original position. Pastels were used for this rabbit portrait. Notice that blue has been used for the shadows rather than black or brown. This adds variety to the limited range of pastel colors. Pastels reproduce fur well, and tinted pastel paper helps to make a pleasing portrait, too.

▼ **Photo Call**
Photographs of your rabbit can help with details, even if your rabbit is "sitting" for his portrait.

1 Sketch the shape of the animal with light pastel strokes. Look carefully at the proportions of the head and body.

2 Use yellow, brown, and white pastels to draw the fur. Make quick, short strokes.

3 Be daring. The dark patches of fur can be drawn in with dark blue strokes.

4 To blend the pastels, use your finger to rub across the marks of color. But be gentle when touching the colors or they will become a muddy mixture.

5 To soften the outline or lines of limbs, flick a brush very gently over the color. Blow away any loose powder onto some newspaper.

▼ **Resting Rabbit**
A dark shadow around the bottom of the animal makes it "sit" on the page. A few strokes of straw indicate his nest. Spray the finished pastel drawing with hair spray to stop it from rubbing off.

Out on the Street

There are more exciting subjects for you to draw and paint out on the street. We live in buildings, shop in them, and work in them, so they make an obvious subject to paint. But not every town road or city street is a safe place from which to study the world. You may have to draw and paint at a distance – from a window looking out on the street, or from a car. Quick sketches can be made from a bus or as you wait for a train.

Sometimes buildings seem too big to fit on the page. And, if you do fit them on, they look out of proportion. Luckily there are some "tricks" to learn that will help you make your cityscapes look real. These tricks include simple rules of perspective that will show you how to draw space and distance, and how to keep your drawing in scale. Once you have mastered simple perspective and can draw the structure of street life, then all you need to do is add those details that make our streets so lively — the people, dogs, cars, bicycles, and so on.

Armed with these tricks, you will find your village, town or city a much more interesting place to draw and paint.

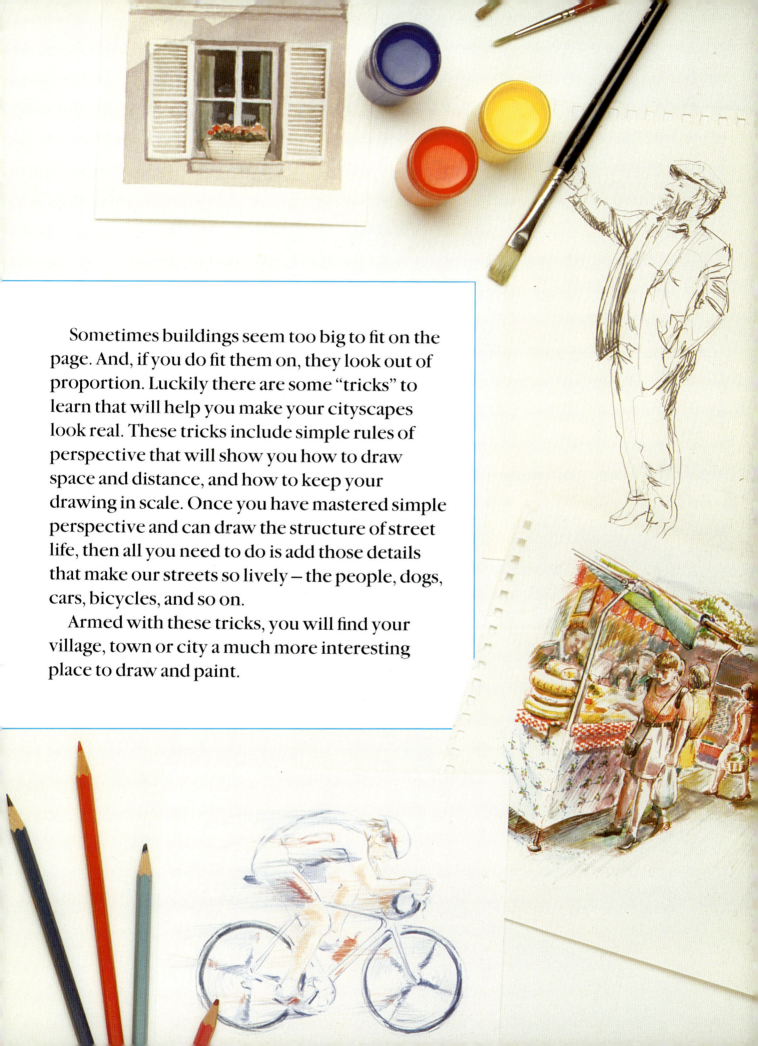

One-Point Perspective

Perspective will help you draw buildings and streets so that the eye travels into the picture, rather than across it. Put in the horizon line (where the sky meets the flat land) at your eye level. This will be high or low depending on whether you are standing or sitting. Then make all horizontal parallel lines, say the sides of the street, run to a point on the horizon called the vanishing point.

◢ Center of the Street
Lines meet at a point on the horizon. Above eye level, they move down; below, they move up.

◢ Side View
Move to one side of the street and the point on the horizon at which the lines vanish, the vanishing point, moves with you.

Drawing Buildings

Look carefully at any street scene. You will notice that distant buildings appear smaller than buildings close to you, even if they are really about the same size. You need to remember this when you are drawing them. There are some simple rules to help you give a sense of distance to your pictures – the rules of perspective.

◢ Getting It Wrong
Because the artist here has not understood how perspective works, the picture looks muddled and unreal. You cannot imagine walking down this street.

◢ Getting It Right
Here, you feel that you could amble down the road to the house at the end. All the horizontal parallel lines, that is those that are an equal distance apart (the top and bottom of the wall, for instance), meet at the vanishing point.

Two-Point Perspective

When you are drawing a building from one corner so that you can see two sides of it, you will need to use two-point perspective.

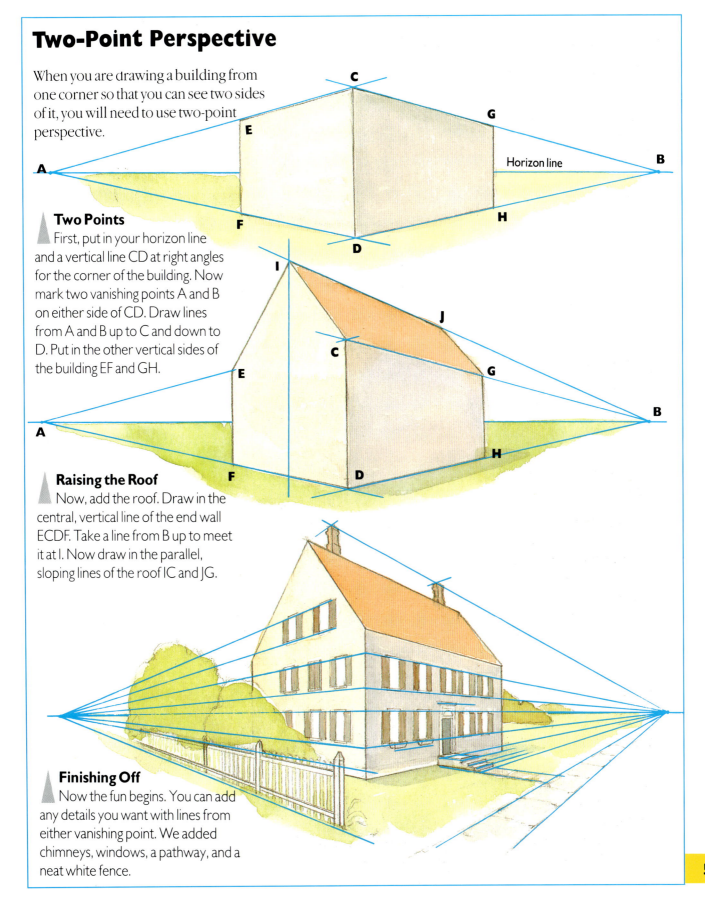

Horizon line

Two Points
First, put in your horizon line and a vertical line CD at right angles for the corner of the building. Now mark two vanishing points A and B on either side of CD. Draw lines from A and B up to C and down to D. Put in the other vertical sides of the building EF and GH.

Raising the Roof
Now, add the roof. Draw in the central, vertical line of the end wall ECDF. Take a line from B up to meet it at I. Now draw in the parallel, sloping lines of the roof IC and JG.

Finishing Off
Now the fun begins. You can add any details you want with lines from either vanishing point. We added chimneys, windows, a pathway, and a neat white fence.

Brickwork

You do not have to paint in every brick in a wall. You just need to give an impression. Try sponging on watercolor to create this effect.

1 Apply a wash of red-brown over sketched brickwork. Now darken the odd brick with more layers of color.

2 Once dry, dip a sponge in brown paint and dab it over the brickwork. This creates the mottled texture of brick.

3 With a fine brush and brown paint, mark in the lines – not every one, and not ruler-straight.

House Portraits

When you paint a house, it is rather like doing a portrait of a person. You need to look at the small details that make it different from other houses – the brickwork, tiles on the roof, or window boxes. Your close observation of these details, and of the fall of light and shade on the building, will give your picture life and form.

Window Study
The more you study details, the more you learn which lines are important to the form and which lines you can leave out. For example, before you plan a painting of a building, study a window. Then, when you paint the whole house, you will know which few important lines you need to hint at the form of the window. This study reveals more than just shutters and frames. It depicts the fall of shadows, the color reflections in glass panes, and the curtains. Go outside and focus in on a window in your home, or stay inside and paint a neighbor's window.

Painting a Portrait

Try painting a portrait of a house you know and like well – maybe your own. Work out the perspective (see pages 58–59) and then add the details.

Roof Shadows
The shadow cast by the gable gives form to this part of the roof.

Window Reflections
A row of windows, but each one different. The reflections add variety.

Economy of Detail
See how this picket fence is only hinted at with clever touches of green.

Light Steps
The fall of light is important even in details like the steps.

People Outdoors

People outdoors are usually on the move – shopping, rushing along, jogging, or walking. You have seen how to capture movement on pages 42–43. Now you can learn to draw people moving around outdoors as part of a larger composition. As you will see, there are various artists' tricks to indicate action.

Giants or Pygmies?

The way we see is strange. Things change depending on the point from which you look at them. Even the tallest person looks short if he is far away. Use perspective lines (see pages 58–59) to fit humans into the scale of buildings and streets.

Whizzing Along
Motion lines, showing the direction of movement, give a strong impression of air rushing past the cyclist as he pedals forward with great speed.

Speeding Along
With this speedy skateboarder, the color has been allowed to "bleed" outside the outline behind her. It has an effect similar to motion lines (above).

Cut for Action

There is a very clever tip that will help you give a strong feeling of movement to the people in your pictures. If a body is "cut" by the frame, it looks as if that body is moving away, right out of the picture. Or perhaps it is moving into the picture, leaving a feeling of space beyond the frame.

People Practice
Before starting on a scene with figures in it, like the market below, you might like to sketch a few possible characters – such as this merchant and woman shopper.

Market Scene
Your sketchbook should be full of people moving through streets or markets with notes about scale and perspective. Now is the time to compose a more finished sketch, like this market scene in colored stylist pens.

Moving Crowd
Here bodies are half bodies. Some are reduced to just head and shoulders as the frame cuts into them. This is how a crowd moves.

One Way
Because there is only one line of movement in this scene, your eye is drawn horizontally across the picture.

Action Angles
Angled, receding lines of perspective, combined with a half figure cut by the frame, give a strong feeling of movement.

Project: Marathon

Now you are ready to tackle a crowd scene and put your new skills to practice. After all, you have sketched lots of figures and can create an impression of people moving with just a few well-chosen lines. This project is worked in gouache. The colors are strong and suit the bold approach of the artist. It is easy to correct mistakes with this medium, by letting each color dry before working over it. The street has a sharp perspective which, coupled with the frame cutting the figures in the foreground, makes it seem as if the runners are bursting forward out of the picture. The artist worked from both sketches and photographs.

▼ Running Figure
In a crowd scene, you won't need detailed studies of each figure. But, by making such drawings, you will learn to refine the line down to the few important ones needed.

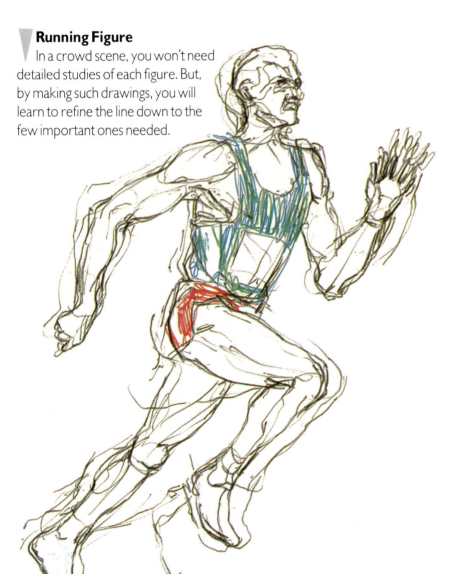

1 Put a paper frame around your picture to keep the edges clean. Now with a fine brush and black paint, outline the running figures. Make them all different, with more detail in the foreground.

2 Indicate buildings with a flat, gray paint. For leafy trees, paint green areas. Then take a sponge, dip it in yellow-green, and sponge over.

3 Fill in flesh tones on faces (see pages 44–45 for color hints). In the foreground, paint arms and legs too. The black outline is important, so paint carefully.

4 Next, add the clothing and flags. Not every detail, just a quick dab here for a red cap, and a touch of yellow there for a T-shirt. Use clear colors to enliven the scene.

5 Now lift the paper frame away. Your painting will have sharp, clean edges and be ready to exhibit.

▲ Motion Picture
With a few black lines and clever patches of paint, you have created a scene that is busy and full of movement. You have had to work fast because gouache dries quickly, but the end result is worth your effort.

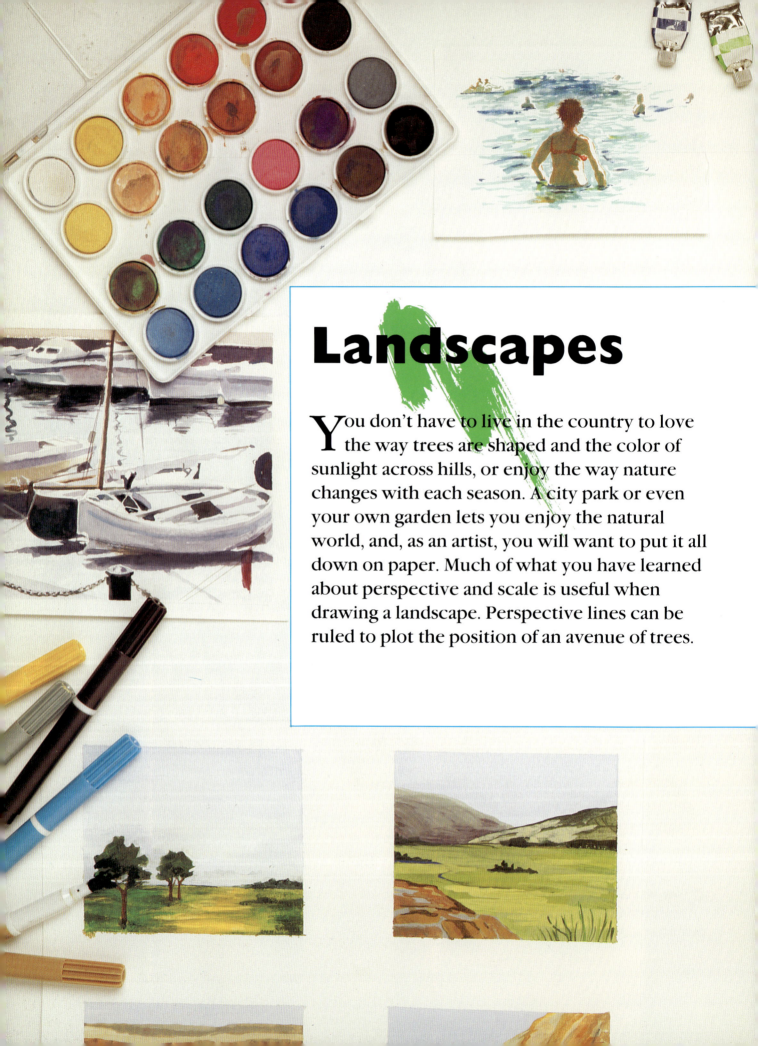

Landscapes

You don't have to live in the country to love the way trees are shaped and the color of sunlight across hills, or enjoy the way nature changes with each season. A city park or even your own garden lets you enjoy the natural world, and, as an artist, you will want to put it all down on paper. Much of what you have learned about perspective and scale is useful when drawing a landscape. Perspective lines can be ruled to plot the position of an avenue of trees.

But you will notice new things — that colors and textures change over distance and that perspectives seem different — because there is more sky and wider space in the country. The sky plays an important part in a landscape. It can often take up half your painting. The more you study the sky and clouds, the more you will find to inspire you. Clouds can be a subject in themselves — angry storm clouds or wispy summer clouds in a blue sky.

If you need photographs of the countryside to paint from, try magazine advertisements. They can give you ideas for dramatic combinations of weather, season, and landscape.

Open Spaces

In a landscape the rules of perspective are still important. Trees get smaller as they disappear into the distance, so you can use perspective lines to work out their relative heights. But there are other ways of creating space in your landscape painting, such as with color and tone. Even when you experiment with an imaginary landscape, you will be amazed to see how careful choice of color changes your work.

Far Horizon
You are high up. The horizon is far away and high on your page. The eye is taken to the horizon, not through receding lines, but through repeated horizontal bands of color.

Natural Scale

How do you fit people into the landscape? The answer is in the same way that you fit them into a city scene – through perspective.

Rule in guiding perspective lines to show the horizon and vanishing point. You will find the right scale when you fit your figures and trees into the lines.

Horizons

The horizon in nature is not always obvious. It is the line where the sky meets the flat land or sea. But the horizon in your picture is still fixed by your eye level. Rules of perspective still apply – below your eye level, lines move up to the horizon. Above eye level, lines move down. And there are vanishing points.

Skyline
The horizon line here is the imaginary one where the sky meets the *flat* land at the end of the plain.

Moving Horizons
The horizon changes when you move. Here the horizon is low down, so you are probably seated.

Low Horizon
To make a dramatic picture, the eye level is low, and the cliffs soar above you.

Making Space

You can use color and tone to help you create a feeling of space in your landscape painting. Strong, warm colors with bright highlights and dark shadows bring objects forward into the foreground. Softer tones and colors take them back.

In this picture, the house is painted in strong red-brown and comes forward from the pale-blue background.

Using the same colors, but reversing their tonal values, the strong blue background now comes forward, pushing the pale house back.

Landscape Colors
Look at this landscape. Notice that cool color is used for distant objects. Things far away from you are more indistinct with a bluish tinge. Things close to you are more detailed and strong in color. Warm colors in the foreground of this landscape bring the objects forward, so that they look as if they are very close to you.

Tree Life

Some artists paint nothing but trees. They are fascinated by their shapes, the movement of the branches in the wind, and the changing appearance of trees through the seasons. On this page, there are some familiar tree shapes, as well as hints about seasonal colors.

Tree Spotting

You will quickly realize that trees often fit into standard geometric shapes, yet each one can be recognized by its unique combination of color and outline. Here are some examples.

Coconut Palm
A coconut palm has wonderful fanlike leaves at the top of a tall trunk. Palm fronds are hard-edged and a strong green.

Cypress Cylinder
Think of the tall shape of the cypress in a cylinder and it will help you to draw it.

Tall Elm
Elms are tall and have strong branches and thick trunks, with a heavy covering of leaves.

Triangular Pine
Many pines such as the Christmas tree are a standard triangle shape.

Blotting and Sponging Leaves

You can give the impression of leaves without painting every one – simply by blotting and sponging. Roughly paint the outline of the foliage with two greens. Quickly, before it dries, blot off excess paint with kitchen tissue. With a sponge, dab in the shadow.

Blowing Blots

This technique is fun and will produce unexpected shapes and color mixtures. When you have made a blown-blot pattern for a tree's leaves and branches, you can paint in a trunk with a brush.

Seasonal Palette

Tree colors and shapes change through the seasons. Look at these examples.

▶ **Winter**
Even though the branches are bare, the tree still has a shape. Give an idea of the network of branches without drawing in every one.

▶ **Spring**
In spring, first the leaves color the branches with a yellow tinge, then, as they grow, the foliage thickens and flowers bloom.

▶ **Summer**
Now the foliage is thick and lush. To give an impression of sunny weather use warm colors.

▶ **Autumn**
For autumn colors, your palette needs brown, ochre, and red paints to mix and capture the season's rich warm tints.

Red + Yellow + Black

Brown + Yellow + Blue   Pink in two tones

Brown + Red   Brown + Yellow

Brown + Yellow   Blue + Yellow + Purple

1 Load your brush with a watery mix of watercolor. Drop a blob on the page and, with a straw blow the paint from the blob.

2 The blob will spread and spatter. You can add other colors and blow, making a rich pattern of colors and textures.

3 Add details with a brush dipped in a dryish paint or use a stylist pen if you prefer.

Skyscapes

When you paint a landscape, the sky often takes up at least half of the picture. Once you start studying the sky, you will find that it is never the same. Even a blue sky is a "cold" blue in winter and a "warm" blue on a hot summer's day. Clouds are always changing. There are techniques to help you capture them.

Winter Mixture
A cold blue for a winter's day. Mix blue with white, or water if you are using watercolor.

Summer Sky
Add a touch of crimson red to the blue to warm it for a summer sky. More red and you will have a sunset sky. But don't overdo it.

Colorful Clouds
Colored grays will make your clouds lively. For cloud shadows, mix blue, brown, and white.

Stormy Weather
Storm clouds and snow clouds can have a yellowish tinge to their shadows.

Cloud Shadows
Use a blue-gray for the shadows of summer clouds in a blue sky. Mix blue with black.

Changing Light
Look how the sky changes throughout the day. The light changes, too.

Morning Sky
Pale, early morning sunlight casts long, soft shadows.

Midday Sky
With the sun high in the sky, shadows are short and dark. The light is hard and bright.

Evening Sky
As the sun sinks, the world is bathed in soft, golden light. Colors fade and shadows lengthen.

Cloud Techniques

Blotting Clouds
For fluffy white clouds, apply a watery wash of blue to your sky. Take a tissue and blot up the color to form white clouds.

Rolling Clouds
Use acrylic paint to apply a flat blue sky. When dry, load your brush with thick white paint and roll the brush over the blue. Add highlights.

Running Clouds
Apply a watery, watercolor blue to an area of sky. While the paint is wet, add gray, then black. The colors run into each other to make storm clouds.

Driving Rain
Apply layers of wet washes so that they run into each other, then blot them with tissue. Make the sheets of rain by dabbing with a tissue around the brush end.

Sunburst
Build up this dramatic sunburst with careful, layered washes, working from light to dark. Wait for each layer to dry before painting the next.

73

Making Waves

Foaming Seas
For waves, build up watery tempera paint, pale green to dark blue. Then layer over thick white paint and use the end of a brush to "sgraffito" (scratch) the movement of the foam.

Rippling Waves
With a thin brush, make a series of irregular, curvy lines in black tempera paint. When dry, fill the spaces between curves with tones of bright and pale blue, and gray.

Clear Water
Clear, clean water, such as you may find in a swimming pool, is painted here with washes then squiggles of blue and green – patterns of deep and bright tones.

Water

Water is like a mirror. It reflects on its surface everything around it – grass, trees, sky, and clouds. Like clouds, water is always moving and changing. Look at the difference between a flat pond, a running river, and wave-tossed seas. You can be really experimental and creative when you paint and draw water. Have fun with colors, techniques, and shapes.

Black Reflections
Here, the reflections of boats are colored in black against washes of blues and gray.

Sunny Reflections
Colored pencil has been used in this scene. Violet, greens, and browns make up sunny, colored reflections.

Strong Light
Short, lively strokes with a felt-tip pen capture the water movement on the sea. Areas of shadow are washed with a wet brush, smoothing out the colors. Unpainted white areas increase a feeling of heat and glare.

Photo Reminder
A photograph of a scene you are painting always helps to jog the memory. But remember, it is best to look at the real thing.

Windy Water
Look how water changes even in a garden pond. Here the wind is blowing and clouds in a blue sky are reflected on the broken surface. Paint in the different colors while each is still wet, letting them merge.

Still Water
Now the surface of the pond is flat and the only movement is caused by the toad. A dull light allows you to see the weeds below the surface. Add white to highlight the ripples.

Project: Tree Study

A garden or park offers a whole range of inspiring subjects to paint and draw. Try to find something simple, like this stately line of trees. You will notice how the artist has used some of the landscape "tricks" you have learned. Perspective lines through the trees meet at a point on the horizon.

Colored pencils are excellent for creating textures with hatched lines, built up in layers. The artist works from light to dark, starting with yellow highlights and building up to heavy, hatched, pencil shadows. Note how the changed direction of hatched strokes adds movement.

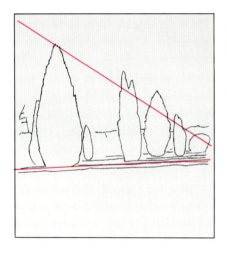

1 With a lead pencil, make a light sketch of the composition. It might help if you start by ruling in lines of perspective for the trees.

2 Loose strokes of light blue fill the sky. Softly hatch pale yellow and light green on the sunny side of the trees.

3 With the side of the pencil, crosshatch layers of brown and dark yellow in the background. You can always darken the tones later.

4 Now add more color to the trees. With short, hatching strokes, go from light green to dark blue. To give movement, vary the stroke direction.

5 Use a ruler to find the straight lines of tree shadows. Then using your dark blue, hatch even strokes against the ruler edge.

6 Loose, free strokes in dark and light green and dark blue create the grassy foreground. Don't cover the paper, as in the sky, but leave some white spaces.

Tree Line
Stand back from your finished picture. You may find you need to deepen a shadow or add a touch of yellow highlight, but be careful not to "overwork" your drawing.

Beyond the Brush

Sometimes a brush just isn't enough! And neither is a pencil. Here, we introduce you to some new ways of working and give you suggestions for original combinations of techniques you already know. Try out everything to see what ideas you can come up with. There are all sorts of things you can do with paint and other media to create a wide variety of unusual effects.

Try adding scraps of material to your landscape. A portrait to paint? How about using a sponge to do it instead of a brush? Fill your paintings with spattering, ragging, and rubbings to show textures — a stony beach or the bark of a tree. These special effects are fun to do and will make your paintings dynamic and unique. Some of the collaging techniques shown on the following pages can be put to use to make an impressive wildlife poster.

Finally, you are invited to explore beyond the real world you can see around you to the realms of ideas and feelings. Subjects like this, which exist only in your mind, free you to express yourself with just color and form.

Two stages of development in a you...

Collage Craft

Collage is fun. It is the art of sticking various materials onto a backing sheet to make a work of art. You can use virtually anything – foil, dried pasta, dried beans, sequins, string, paper clips. See what you can find. Use a household glue, not paper paste, and collage onto a sheet of thick paper or cardboard. Add paint or penwork, but let the glue dry first.

Paper Waves

1 Collage can be used for some quite ambitious projects, like this seascape. Make clouds by tearing and cutting black tissue.

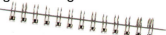

Rosy Picture
Sometimes the materials you have found for your collage will suggest an idea to you. Otherwise go through your sketchbook or ideas file for something to try.

Paper Rose
Draw the shapes you need onto colored paper and cut or tear them out. Torn paper has a soft edge, so use it for the rose petals and leaves. Lay out these shapes before you glue them.

Waxy Rose
The petals of this rose collage were outlined with pen and paint. Some of the leaves are textured by scratching into a layer of crayon.

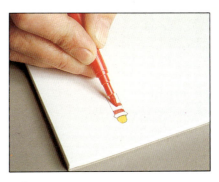

2 Now for the distant waves, fold a piece of paper over three or four times. Cut holes into the folds. Open up and glue the paper below the clouds.

3 The larger waves in front are made by cutting curved pieces of plain colored paper, then tearing up sheets of speckled blue paper to make wave crests.

4 You might not find all the elements you want in torn or cut paper. Draw what you need – a lighthouse perhaps – cut it out and glue it on.

Stormy Sea
The finished picture is a pleasing mix of hard and soft edges, unusual textures and colors. The collage technique works well here.

Looking at Texture

Rough, smooth, knobbly, spiked – the the world is full of strange and wonderful textures. Of course, you do not have to use an ordinary paintbrush to capture these extraordinary surfaces. You can paint with your fingers, with rags, tissues, and sponges.

Leaf Prints

You can make colorful leaf patterns by printing the shapes of real leaves. Use a new leaf for each color.

1 Use acrylic or tempera paint. Apply a thick layer to the upper side of the leaf. Start with a small leaf, one with an interesting shape.

2 Press the leaf on the paper firmly with the paint side down. Then peel it off quickly. Place one leaf print over another or overlap the prints.

Ragging
For a leafy path or a tree trunk, try ragging. The idea is to dab a scrunched-up rag dipped in a dry, dark color over dry washes of pale color.

Sponging
This pebble is built up with layers of sponging. Use a fine sponge and dry paint. Start with dark gray and finish with white. Cut a mask for the edge to keep it clean.

Blotting
To make subtle changes within a wash of color, use the blotting technique. After you have applied your color, soak off patches with a piece of tissue twisted into a point.

82

Spattering
Dip a toothbrush into paint, then pull your thumb back over the bristles, spattering the paint across the page. Mask with paper any areas you want to keep clean. You can see how this technique has been used for the beach area below.

Rubbing It In

This is a technique that is well-suited to collage but, of course, it can be part of any painted picture.

1 Lay a piece of paper over a textured surface, say stone or wood. Rub over the paper with a pencil or crayon.

2 Move the paper slightly and rub again with another color. Stick this rubbing on drawing paper, then paint and draw over it.

Good Impressions

With this technique it is hard to tell what is going to happen. You paint onto one surface with thick paint, then press a sheet of paper on top. Use a "print" like this to add texture to an area of flat paint.

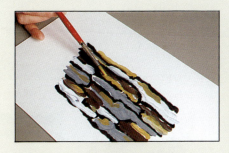

1 With thick tempera paint, build up an image of a wall. Do this quickly or the paint will dry.

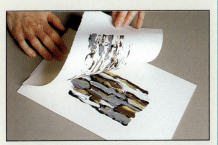

2 Place a sheet of paper over the top and press down over the painted area. The more you press, the more blurred the image will be.

Using Photographs

It is exciting to sketch from life. Fortunately, we all have the opportunity to study birds and many of us can draw from living insects. But we can't always copy from life. Few of us can go on a safari to look at giraffes or tigers. Also, animals, birds, and insects move around so often, it is hard to sketch them. So photographs can really help to increase our knowledge of animals' bodies and movements. Look in magazines and books, and collect cuttings for your reference sketchbook.

Bird Shapes
Try to see the shapes of birds as you sketch. Match them to geometric shapes (see pages 20–21.) Using photographs to draw from will make it easy to see these shapes and get them right.

In-Flight Pictures
You need to sketch quickly when a pigeon or seabird flies by. Build your confidence by studying photos. This will help you when you draw from life.

▷ Paper Bird

This seagull was drawn from a newspaper cutting. Black-and-white photographs often give a clearer idea of an animal's shape, as color can distract you.

◁ Look to Learn

Look for photographs that show different aspects of a bird, animal, or insect. This helps you to understand how its body "works."

A Photocopier

To help you copy, or enlarge, the subject of a photograph, you can make a grid from a piece of tracing paper, which can be used again and again.

1 On tracing paper, make a grid of equal squares to fit over the photo. Use a permanent pen to mark the lines.

2 Place this grid over the photograph you want to copy. Fix it with masking tape, then follow the instructions on enlarging (page 29).

◁ Lively Locust

Using the three magazine photographs of a locust you can see above, the artist has made a study in colored pencils. Different photographs were useful for different aspects of the study.

85

Project: Wildlife Poster

This project uses many of the techniques covered in the previous pages. There is a bit of collage, work from photographs, and some texture techniques. All these combine to make a poster that gives a lot of information through artwork not words. But first you need to gather as much information as possible about a particular animal that interests you. Then you can build up a "catalogue" of your studies in the form of a poster. You might like to try this for school projects. One advantage to this project is that you can prepare numerous drawings and paintings of the subject, then select the best ones to cut out and use in the finished work. Your poster could show a favorite animal or bird, or a study of wildflowers. The subject chosen here was the life cycle of the frog.

1 Draw the frog's outline and main features on a piece of green paper and cut them out.

2 Make a tracing of the pink parts on its head, legs, and underside. Trace them onto pink paper and cut them out.

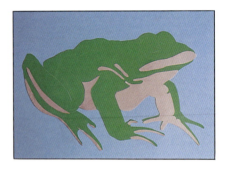

3 Assemble all the cut pieces on a blue background sheet and glue them on carefully with paper glue.

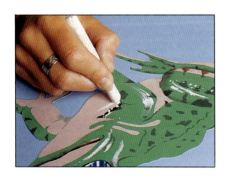

4 Draw the details of the frog's markings onto the paper cut-outs with crayons and pastels. Make the shapes and colors clear and bold.

5 Do the developing tadpole sketches for the poster on separate sheets of paper, using paint, crayon, or pastel.

6 Cut out the smaller drawings and arrange them on a sheet of white cardboard, together with the cut-out frog. When the arrangement looks good, glue on the pieces.

A FROG'S LIFE

The tiny new frog hops out of the pond.

The tadpoles' tails shrink and their bodies grow bigger.

Frogs often sit on the flat lily pads.

Next they grow front legs.

The tadpoles grow back legs.

The tadpoles hatch out of the spawn.

In the spring, female frogs lay eggs, called spawn, in the pond.

A Frog's Life
A poster like this displays the whole of the frog's life cycle from spawn and tadpole to adult. To finish it, the artist has added handwritten labels.

Project: Jungle Impression

You may long to express your thoughts just in color, or paint the mood of a place, not only how it looks. If you do you will be painting an abstract. An abstract painting usually has no people or things you can recognize in it, only colors and shapes, which express the artist's ideas and feelings. But you can go halfway to an abstract, as in this project. The artist wanted to paint a tropical jungle. As you see, it is not an exact copy, but uses leaf shapes and colors that suggest tropical vegetation. The picture gives an impression of a jungle. Using your imagination try the same scene yourself with leaf patterns, collage, fragments of glittery fabric, or magazine photographs of tropical plants and trees.

Local Inspiration
These houseplants inspired the shapes of the forest plants and leaves in this project. There may be something in your home – an ornament or a flower – that gives you the idea for an imaginary place.

1 Sketch in the basic shapes of the large leaves and use wax resist (see pages 32–33) to create the bright green and white pattern.

2 Use oil pastels to fill in the dark background areas. Because these are greasy, they make a surface that resists paint in the same way as candle wax does.

3 Apply washes of acrylic paint very broadly into each of the main color areas. You can brush one color over another to make color changes.

4 Use thicker paint to darken heavy shadows in the background behind the trees. You can brush it over the oil pastel color used in Step 2.

5 Put in the smaller shapes by painting real leaves and using them as leaf prints (see pages 82–83). You can print them in one color or multicolors – use the same technique but apply two or three different colors to one leaf.

6 Add details like these small white flowers by sponging little dabs of thick tempera paint over the darker areas already painted. Make sure the paint underneath has dried first, or the colors will run, making the white muddy.

▲ Tropical Trees

The artist has given the impression of a lush jungle with a few shapes and powerful color. The tree trunks and large leaves of the background come alive with the broken textures of wax and oil pastel resist. Overall, the painting combines a lot of the techniques you have learned, so you should be able to achieve something just as good!

Glossary

A

acrylic paint A kind of paint that has a thick, moist texture and comes in a range of bright colors. It can be mixed and thinned with water, but becomes waterproof when dry.

B

bleeding A technique in which color is washed over the outline of a drawing to increase the feeling of movement.

blending A technique in which one color is merged into another. In painting, you can brush the colors together while they are still wet. Using colored pencils, the colors are shaded into one another.

blotting A technique for lightening colors in a painting by lifting wet paint with a tissue or rag.

burnishing A technique in which a final layer of white pencil is shaded over a colored-pencil drawing to blend and "polish" the colors.

C

cast shadow A shadow made when a solid shape blocks the light. The dark shadow of a standing object or figure, for example, is cast onto the wall or floor.

chalk pastel A drawing material made from pigment and gum mixed together and rolled into stick form, then allowed to harden. Chalk pastel is completely dry and becomes loose and crumbly when pressed hard.

collage A technique of making pictures by gluing on paper shapes and other materials that can be cut or torn from different sources. The resulting picture is also called a collage.

composition The arrangement or design of a picture. Elements of composition include lines, shapes, colors, tones, patterns, and textures.

crosshatching A drawing technique for creating areas of color and tone by making patterns of closely spaced parallel lines going in opposite directions.

D

dry brush A painting technique that enables an artist to make a fine, "hairy" texture by spreading out the hairs of a brush between finger and thumb and dragging it through paint.

E

ellipse An oval shape, which is the way a circle looks when you see it on a slant or at an angle.

enlarging A method of copying a picture in a larger size. It is done by drawing a grid over the original picture, then copying the shapes in each square onto a larger grid.

F

flat color An area of a painting that is the same color all over, and does not show any brush marks or shading.

foreground The area, or plane, in a picture that is nearest to the viewer. A picture can usually be divided into three main planes: the foreground which is closest to you, the middle ground, and the background in the distance.

G

gouache A type of paint made from a gum binder, pigment, and a white "filler" material like chalk. Gouache paint is smooth, thick, and opaque.

gummed tape Brown paper tape that has a thin coating of gum on one side. When you wet it, it becomes very sticky and adheres firmly when it dries.

H

highlight The brightest point or area on an object, where light is reflected most strongly.

horizon line A dividing line in a painting or drawing that represents the farthest point you can see. For example, in a landscape painting, it is the line between ground and sky. In perspective drawing it is the line (sometimes imaginary) where the sky meets the *flat* land.

M

modeling In drawing and painting, the method of using light and shadow (by blending or shading, for example) to make the picture look three-dimensional and real.

O

oil pastel A drawing material that consists of pigment mixed with an oil binder shaped into sticks of color.

opaque The description of something that cannot be seen through, the opposite of transparent.

P

palette The dish, board, or flat slab on which an artist lays out colors to be thinned and mixed for painting. The word is also used to mean the range of colors that an artist uses in a painting.

perspective The drawing method used by artists to show space, distance, and solidity in a picture, converting a view of the three-dimensional world into a two-dimensional image.

pigment The ingredient of a paint that gives it color.

portrait A painting or drawing that shows a recognizable likeness of a human subject, so that you can tell who the person is by looking at the picture. The term can also be applied to pets and non-living things, such as houses.

proportions The sizes of different parts of a figure or object in relation to one another.

R

reflection The appearance of color and light on a surface that comes from a separate surface or object. Sometimes it may be a flash of light, as in a highlight on a shiny surface. Or it could be a whole picture, as seen in a mirror.

rubbings Drawings made by laying paper over a textured surface and rubbing with a crayon.

S

scale The sizes and locations of different things in relation to one another. For example, in a landscape view, a mountain or cliff is a large-scale object, whereas flowers and blades of grass are small-scale features. But if the pictured mountain is far away, it might appear quite small, while a flower close to you could appear large by comparison.

sgraffito A technique in which lines are scratched, for example with a brush end or pin, into paint to reveal the paper underneath.

shading In drawing, the technique of creating areas of light or dark colors and tones, and blends between them, by rubbing the pencil tip evenly over the paper.

sketch A drawn or painted picture done quickly to give an impression of the subject, rather than a detailed study.

spattering A painting technique in which wet color is flicked off the bristles of a brush with a finger or thumb to make a pattern of dots and splashes.

sponging A painting technique in which paint is applied with a small piece of sponge rather than a brush to create mottled textures.

still life An arrangement of non-living objects that forms the subject of a painting or drawing, for example, cups and pitchers, fruits or vegetables. The term is also used to describe the resulting picture.

study A detailed painting or drawing of a subject. A study is usually a more highly finished picture than a sketch.

T

tempera paint A type of inexpensive paint, similar to gouache, which is thick and opaque.

three-dimensional The quality of the real world, which contains open spaces and solid objects that you can move through and around. A drawing or painting is two-dimensional, that is, flat, so artists have to use methods such as perspective drawing and modeling to re-create three-dimensional effects.

tone A degree of lightness or darkness. In drawing and painting, tone is a measure of relative values – for example, on a scale from white through gray to black.

transparent color Color that can be seen through when put on the paper, like that applied with crayons or watercolor paints.

W

wash A thin layer of transparent color, made by mixing paint with water and brushing it on thinly.

watercolor A type of paint made from pigment mixed with a gum binder. It dissolves easily in water, and is available in moist and hard forms, packaged in tubes or pans.

wax resist A combined drawing and painting technique in which a wax candle or crayon is used to draw, then a wash of paint color is brushed over the top. The paint cannot settle on the wax, so it flows around the drawing to form a background color.

Index

93